Success with Phonics

Letters and Sounds

Workbook 8

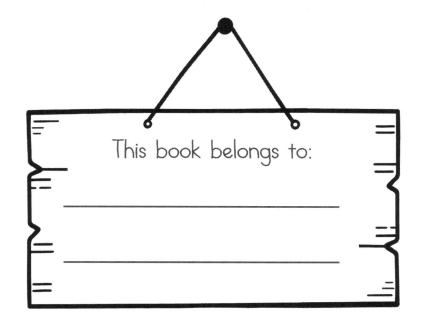

This book belongs to:

_____

_____

Quail Publishers

About the Series

Quail Publishers' *Success with Phonics* series offers parents and educators comprehensive, high quality, curriculum-based products that are aligned to English language K-2 standards. The program utilizes the Science of Reading components: phonemic awareness, phonics, vocabulary, fluency and comprehension to ensure literacy. The explicit, systematic phonics strategies get children reading and writing from an early age. Each book covers a group of the most common sound-spelling combinations of the English language, with engaging, multi-sensory activities for children to read fluently and confidently.

NOTE

Kindly note the interactive digital copy of this book is available at Quail Publishers on Boom Learning™. To access:

- Sign up for Boom Learning at https://wow.boomlearning.com/
- Choose a plan.
- Go to the store menu.
- Search for Quail Publishers.
- Look for the Success with Phonics boom card sets.
- Purchase decks using Boom's points system.
- Go to library and you will see the decks.

Quail Publishers

Written by Allison Hall. Edited by Keisha Baboolal and Allison Hall
Cover and interior design by Allison Hall | Illustrations: FreePik, Pixabay and Dreamstime
Text Copyright © 2019 by Allison Hall. All rights reserved.
Revised 2022
Published by Quail Publishers LLC, Coral Springs, Florida. www.quailpublishers.com
ISBN: 978-1-7376008-5-5

Table of Contents

Introduction

Studies continue to show that mastery of phonics is a very important first step on the road to learning to read. Through phonics instruction, children learn the relationships between letters (graphemes) of our written language and the individual sounds (phonemes) of spoken language. Once children have mastered short vowel sounds and the most common consonant blends, digraphs and long vowel sound-spelling relationships, they are ready to learn diphthongs and r-controlled sounds.

A diphthong is a letter sound that starts with a vowel sound and glides to another sound, for example /oi/, in the word /coil/. The r-controlled sound on the other hand is when the consonant 'r', often referred to as the bossy 'r', changes the sound of the vowel that precedes it. The new sound is called an r-controlled sound. R-controlled sounds include /ar/ and /or/, which can be heard in the words car and horse respectively. There are also long vowel sounds that are influenced by the consonant 'r'. These r-influenced sounds include /are/, /ere/, /ire/, /ore/ and /ure/. Some programs recognize them as two sounds, whilst others teach them as one. It must also be noted that the long 'u' sound can stand for /ō͞o/ as in chew and /yō͞o/ as in new. Similarly, the letter team 'ure' stands for the sounds /ŏor/ as in lure or /yŏor/ as in pure.

The Activity Sheets

The Success with Phonics: Letters and Sounds Workbook 8 contains worksheets to help children learn other spellings of the most common diphthongs and r-controlled sounds. There are two pages dedicated to teaching each sound. These fully reproducible sheets contain engaging activities that promote the following:

- **Phonemic Awareness**: Identify sounds in spoken words
- **Handwriting**: Write the letters that represent each sound
- **Spelling**:
    * Use picture clues to spell words with the target sound
    * Identify the correct spelling of words with the target sound
- **Reading**: Read simple sentences with the target sound
- **Write**: Write sentences with the target sound

There are also activities to help you review the sounds taught. The workbooks can be used at home and in the classroom and are an excellent supplement to any reading program.

Teaching the Sounds

Teaching letter sounds should be fast-paced, engaging and fun. Here are some suggested steps to teach the sounds and their spellings in this book

Before the Lesson
1. Review the letter sound and main picture you will be teaching.
2. Read other literature on letter sounds and their spellings
3. Develop an exciting and engaging lesson which allows for multi-sensory activities and integrate technology where applicable.
4. Make sure that children have the necessary stationery and resources to participate in the lesson.
5. Ensure lessons have activities to foster home-school connections.
6. Be aware that some children will have more advanced phonics knowledge than others. Use differentiated instruction to meet each student's needs.

Teaching the Lesson

Review: Review previously taught sounds.

Phonemic Awareness - Invite children to listen carefully as you say a picture name with the sound you are teaching. Stress the sound and model the proper mouth position to say the letter sound correctly. For example, say, /**tray**/ and stretch the sound you are teaching. Invite children to say the picture name also, and identify the letter sound in words.

Phonics—Write the word on the board. For example, write the word 'tray' on the board. Use sound buttons (●) to show the number of sounds in each word. An extended button or line (_____) shows a digraph or trigraph, or the r-influenced sound. The curved line with a sound button (⌣) represents a split digraph. Explain the phonics concept being taught, that the letters 'ay' is another spelling of the long 'a' sound. Next, invite children to say the sound, being taught two times, then write the letters that stand for the sound on their worksheets.

Word Building - Have children spell words and read sentences with the sound being taught

Revision - Review constantly until children have mastered this phonics principle.

Assessment - Use authentic assessment to measure students' progress.

High Frequency Words

High frequency words are those words that appear most frequently in texts. These words include, 'and', 'I', 'is', 'the', 'can' and 'to'. Children must learn these words very early in order to read sentences automatically, accurately and fluently. Some high frequency words can be decoded easily, as they follow the regular spelling rules. However, some have tricky parts that do not follow the regular spelling rules and can be a challenge for young readers. These irregularly spelled words are called sight words, as it is expected that children should *read them when they see them*. There are also some words, such as 'her' and 'like', that do not have an irregular spelling pattern. However, they must be taught as sight words, as children are not yet introduced to their sounds and spellings.

Read-Write-Spell

The Success with Phonics program uses the Read-Write-Spell strategy to teach sight or tricky words. Here some steps to teach sight words using this strategy.

- Say the sight word being taught three times. Ask children to repeat the word twice.
- Invite children to sound out the letters in the word.
- Discuss the irregular, or tricky part of the word (*where the letter does not correspond to the sound, or sounds children associate with that letter*).
- Have children trace the word, after which they will spell the word on their own.
- Write the sight word on a card and place it on a word wall. Color-code the word, to remind children of the tricky part. Children should write it in their word bank.
- Refer to it regularly throughout the day, so that by the end of the day children learn the word. Always review the word until children learn it.

Reinforcement Strategies

Word Wall
A word wall is a great tool that supports phonics instruction. It is a display of words, or word parts, that is used to teach spelling, reading and writing. Mount words with the sound-spelling being taught on a wall as reinforcement.

Word Bank
A word bank is a great way for children to improve their vocabulary, create a word list, reinforce alphabetical order and memorize the spelling of unfamiliar words. Children may use a notebook to create their word banks. Have them devote a sheet of paper for each letter. At the top of each page, they should write each letter in its upper and lower-case forms. Ensure that they start with letters 'Aa', as the bank should be arranged in alphabetical order. Children should place new words they have learned in their bank.

Name _____   Date _____

The Long 'A' Sound
Say the picture name. Listen for the last sound. Say the sound.

ay 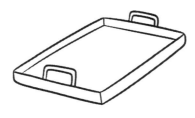 tray
___

Spelling
Write the letters 'ay' to complete the spelling of the words. Color the pictures.

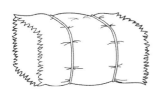

h_____   j_____   cr_____on

Reading
Read the words and sentence below. Write a sentence in your notebook with one of the words.

say   may   day

play   stay   pray

May I play in the hay?

The Long 'E' Sound

Say the picture name. Listen for the middle sound. Say the sound.

ea  leaf

Spelling

Write the letters 'ea' to complete the spelling of the words. Color the pictures.

b_____n   s____l   p_____ch

Reading

Read the words and sentence. Write a sentence in your notebook with one of the words.

eat   teach   read

seat   meal   steam

Mean Jean ate all the beans.

The Long 'I' Sound

Say the picture name. Listen for the middle sound. Say the sound.

igh

tights

Spelling

Write the letters 'igh' to complete the spelling of the words. Color the pictures.

n_____t   flash l_____t   kn_____t

Reading

Read the words and sentence below. Write a sentence in your notebook with one of the words.

light   night   right

sight   flight   bright

The moon is bright tonight.

The Long 'I' Sound

Say the picture name. Listen for the last sound. Say the sound. The consonant 'y' also stands for the long 'i' sound.

y   fly

Spelling

Write the letters 'y' to complete the spelling of the words. Color the pictures.

sk____   st_____   dr_____er

Reading

Read the words and sentence below. Write a sentence in your notebook with one of the words.

my   by   dry

try   cry   why

Why is the pig sty so dry?

The Long 'O' Sound

Say the picture name. Listen for the last sound. Say the sound.

OW

 snow

Spelling

Write the letters 'ow' to complete the spelling of the words. Color the pictures.

b_____

cr_____

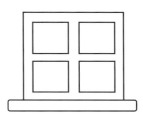

wind_____

Reading

Read the words and sentence below. Write a sentence in your notebook with one of the words.

low   row   bow

grow   show   blow

The bow fell in the snow.

Name _____ Date _____

The Long 'O' Sound

Say the picture name. Listen for the last sound. Say the sound. The letters 'oe' can stand for the long 'o' sound.

oe  hoe

---

Spelling

Write the letters 'oe' to complete the spelling of the words. Color the pictures.

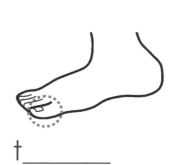 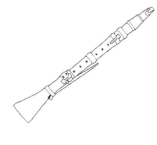 

t_____   ob_____   domin_____s

Reading

Read the words and sentence. Write a sentence in your notebook with one of the words.

toe   foe   doe

goes   woe   aloe

The hoe fell on Joe's toe.

          Success with Phonics: Letters and Sounds Workbook 8

The Long 'U' Sound

Say the picture name. Listen for the long 'u' sound. Say the sound.

  stat**ue**

Spelling

Write the letters 'ue' to complete the spelling of the words. Color the pictures.

gl_____

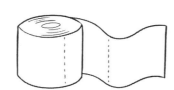

tiss_____

Reading

Read the words and sentence below. Write a sentence in your notebook with one of the words.

due   hue   cue

true   blue   glue

Sue likes blue hues.

The Long 'U' Sound

Say the picture names. Listen for the long 'u' sound in each word. The long 'u' sound can also be spelled with the letter teams 'ew' or 'ui'.

Reading

Read the words below. Then write sentences in your notebook with some of the words.

 screw

new   few   dew   pew

blew   chew   grew   threw

Drew saw a shrew by the pew.

 suit

suit   fruit   bruise

Ray hid the fruit in his suit.

The /oi/ Sound

Say the picture name. Listen for the middle sound. Say the sound.

  coil

Spelling

Write the letters 'oi' to complete the spelling of the words. Color the pictures.

_____ l   f _____ l   c _____ n

Reading

Read the words and sentence below. Write a sentence in your notebook with one of the words.

soil   boil   join

point   spoil   moist

The coil fell in the oil.

Name _____   Date _____

The /ou/ Sound

Say the picture name. Listen for the middle sound. Say the sound.

ou  hou**se**

Spelling

Write the letters 'ou' to complete the spelling of the words. Color the pictures.

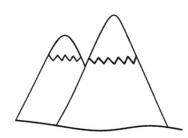

m_____se   m_____ntain   bl_____se

Reading

Read the words and sentence below. Write a sentence in your notebook with one of the words.

mouth   loud   round

shout   about   found

They found the hound lying on the ground.

     Success with Phonics: Letters and Sounds Workbook 8

The /er/ Sound

Say the picture name. Listen for the last sound. Say the sound.

ladd**er**

Spelling

Write the letters 'er' to complete the spelling of the words. Color the pictures.

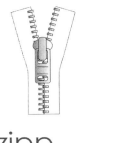      

zipp_____   flow_____   tig_____

Reading

Read the words and sentence below. Write a sentence in your notebook with one of the words.

h**er**   t**er**m   f**er**n

v**er**b   j**er**k   h**er**b

This term I will get a perm.

 **High Frequency Word**

Read
Say the word.

were

Write
Write the word.

were

Spell
Circle the correct spelling of the word.

wer   were   where   were

Trace the word '**were**' to complete the sentence. Read the sentence.

The toys were not in the box.

Write a sentence with the word '**were**'. Then write it in your word bank.

Name _____   Date _____

The /au/ Sound

Say the picture name. Listen for the middle sound. Say the sound.

au ○ s**au**cer

Spelling

Write the letters 'au' to complete the spelling of the words. Color the pictures.

  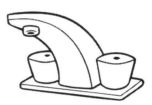

astron_____t   s_____ce   f_____cet

Reading

Read the words and sentence below. Write a sentence in your notebook with one of the words.

haul   taunt   fault

haunt   maul   launch

Paul will haul the sand.

The /au/ Sound

Say the picture name. Listen for the middle sound. Say the sound. The letter 'a' can also stand for the sound /au/.

  ball

Phonics Tip: The letter 'a' usually stands for the sound /au/ when it comes before the letters 'l' or 'll', or after 'w'. For example: also, call and want.

Blending

Blend the sounds to read the words.

all

salt

call

want

also

water

Reading

Read the sentence.

 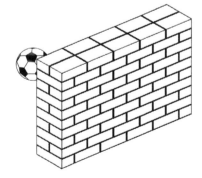

The ball hit the wall.

The /are/ Sound

Say the picture name. Listen for the last sound. Say the sound.

-are 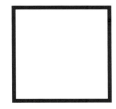 squ**are**

Spelling

Write the letters 'are' to complete the spelling of the words. Color the pictures.

h_____

w_____house

Reading

Read the words and sentence below. Write a sentence in your notebook with one of the words.

care   bare   fare

dare   scare   share

The dogs will scare the hare.

The /ere/ Sound

Say the picture name. Listen for the last sound. Say the sound.

-ere 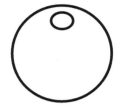 sph**ere**

Reading

Read the words below. Then read the sentences.

w h e r e   t h e r e   h e r e

Reading

Read the sentences.

Where is Tim?
I am **here** mom.
Where is Ron?
Ron is in **there**?
Here am I.

The /eer/ Sound

Say the picture name. Listen for the last sound. Say the sound.

-eer  deer

Spelling

Write the letters 'eer' to complete the spelling of the words. Color the pictures.

b_____   m_____kat   st_____

Reading

Read the words and sentence below. Write a sentence in your notebook with one of the words.

deer   jeer   queer

cheer   steer   sheer

Dad will steer away from the deer.

Name _____   Date _____

The /ire/ Sounds

Say the picture name. Listen for the last sounds. Say the sounds.

-ire

 fire

---

Spelling

Write the letters 'ire' to complete the spelling of the words. Color the pictures.

t_____   w_____   vamp_____

Reading

Read the words and sentence below. Write a sentence in your notebook with one of the words.

tire   wire   hire

sire   dire   squire

The sharp wire cut the umpire.

        Success with Phonics: Letters and Sounds Workbook 8

The /ore/ Sound

Say the picture name. Listen for the last sound. Say the sound.

-ore    store

Spelling

Write the letters 'ore' to complete the spelling of the words. Then read the sentence.

Miss Gore is by the sea_____ .

Reading

Read the words and sentence below. Write a sentence in your notebook with one of the words.

more   tore   wore   core

bore   score   chore   shore

Miss Gore wore a red dress to the store.

The /ore/ Sound

Say the picture names. Listen for the last sound in each word. Say the sound. The sound /ore/ can also be spelled with the letter teams 'oar' or 'oor'.

Reading

Read the words below with the sound. Write sentences in your notebook with some of the words.

-oar

boar

oar   boar   soar   board

The big boar broke the oar.

-oor

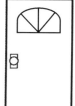

door

floor   moor   poor

The poor man fell on the wet floor.

Success with Phonics: Letters and Sounds Workbook 8

Name _____ Date _____

The /ure/ Sounds
Say the picture name. Listen for the last sounds. Say the sounds.

-ure  manure

Spelling
Write the letters 'ure' to complete the spelling of the words. Then read the sentence.

The man will l____ the rats into the river.

Reading
Read the words and sentence below. Write a sentence in your notebook with one of the words.

cure   pure   mure

secure   mature   endure

Ray had to endure the smell of the manure.

High Frequency Word

Read
Say the word.

sure

Write
Write the word.

sure

Spell
Circle the correct spelling of the word.

sure   soar   sure   shore

Trace the word 'sure' to complete the sentence. Read the sentence.

I am sure the water

is pure.

Write a sentence with the word 'sure'. Then write it in your word bank.

Name _____   Date _____

The /ph/ Sound

Say the picture name. Listen for the first sound. Say the sound.

 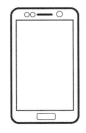 phone

Spelling

Write the letters 'ph' to complete the spelling of the words. Color the pictures.

dol____in   ele____ant   al____abet

Reading

Read the words and sentence below. Write a sentence in your notebook with one of the words.

orphan   graphic   phase

alphabet   sphere

The dolphin has Phil's phone.

High Frequency Words

Read
Read the words.

Write
Trace the words, then add them to your word bank.

Spell
Write the word **any** or **many** to complete the sentences. Read the sentences.

Tim has _____ books in his bag.

Liz did not have _____ lunch.

I have _____ toys.

Sentence Building
Write a sentence using either **any** or **many**.

_____

_____

Find the Words: Say the picture names. Listen carefully for the **sounds** in each word. Then circle the <u>correct</u> spelling of the word.

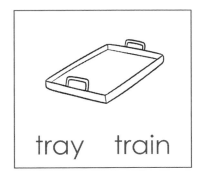

tray   train

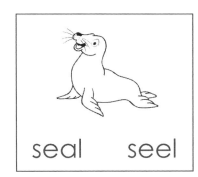

seal   seel

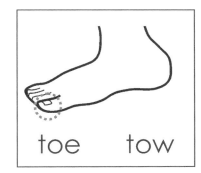

toe   tow

glew   glue

hare   hear

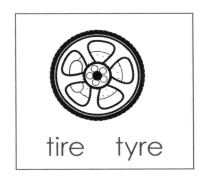

tire   tyre

Fill in the Blanks

Write letter '**e**' on the lines below to complete the words. Then read the sentences with the new words.

Treat the **car** with **car____**.

Her bag is not **her____**.

Is the **fir** tree on **fir____**?

The cap is **for** the **for___**man.

Will the film **star star____** at the moon?

Spelling

- ◆ **Look** carefully at each picture.
- ◆ **Say** the picture name.
- ◆ **Listen** for the sounds in each word.
- ◆ **Write** the letters that represent the sounds. Use the sound buttons (•) to help you. Each stands for one sound. Twin buttons (•—•) stand for a consonant blend. A long line with one button below it stands for a digraph or trigraph(‾•‾).
- ◆ **Read** the word that you have written. Check your spelling.

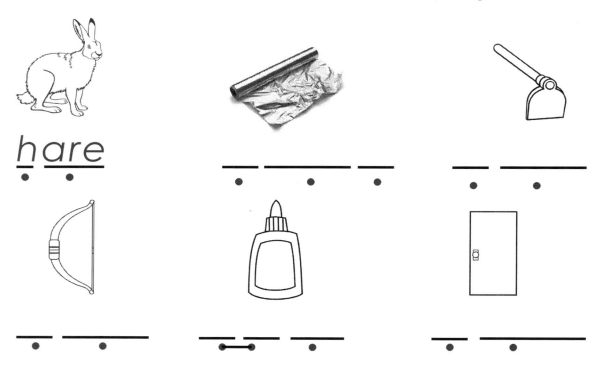

_h_ _are_

Guess the Riddles: Listen carefully as your teacher, or parent, reads the riddles below. Then write the missing letters to complete the spelling of the words.

Grass that is dried.   h_____

A beverage made from leaves.   t_____

You use it to fry food.   _____l

A lack of money, food and shelter.   p_____

Name _____   Date _____

Picture Clues: Use the pictures as clues to help you to spell the missing words. Read the sentences.

1. A p_____ch is a fruit.

2. Sue puts the meal on a tr_____ .

3. My sister did not shut the d_____ .

4. This winter we will get a lot of sn_____.

5. We made a f_____ to keep us warm.

Words that Sound Alike: Some words sound alike, but they have different spelling and meaning. Use the word parts and pictures as clues to help you to spell the words.

ea   ear   are   ore   oor

1. Ray and Sue will <u>mee</u>t at the m_____t shop.

2. I can s<u>ee</u> the s_____ from my window.

3. We could not b<u>are</u> to hear the b_____ growl.

4. I can h<u>ear</u> the h_____ running in the woods.

5. Drew was <u>sure</u> that he left his hat by the seash_____.

Name _____   Date _____

Comprehension: Read the passage and answer the questions.

Farmers' Market

It is Saturday! Sue and Paul are at the farmers' market. Paul's mother is a farmer. Sue will help Paul to sell the crops his mother grew. The market is full of people. Stalls with rows of green, blue, yellow and red. Food for all to be well fed.

Paul's mother has a small stall. But there are fresh foods for all. She has peppers, cloves of garlic and carrots. And yams, nuts and fruits too. The end of the day is the best part. The children will visit the new stalls and shops. They will thank the farmers for the crops.

Write the correct words on the lines to complete each sentence.

1.   On which day is the farmers' market held?
      The farmers' market is held on a _____.

2.   What will Paul and Sue sell at the farmers' market?
      Paul and Sue will sell _____

      _____

3.   What will the children do at the end of the day?
      The children will _____

      _____

Discussion
1.   What is a farmers' market?
2.   Why is it held on a particular day?
3.   How does it help farmers?

Name _____   Date _____

Community Helpers: The word part '**er**' is often added to action words to form naming words or nouns. Some of these nouns name workers in our communities who do important jobs. Add the word part '**er**' to the action words below to make nouns.

teach____

paint____

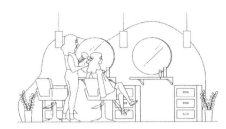

hairdress____

farm____

clean____

firefight____

When I Grow-up: Write a sentence to tell others of the type of job you would like to do when you grow up. Make a community helper scrap book.

When I grow up I
I would like to be

Syllables: Some words have one or more groups of sounds called syllables. Sometimes syllables are called beats. Each syllable has a vowel sound. Read the words below that have two beats or syllables.

1. Blend the sounds to read the first part of the word.
2. Then blend the sounds to read the second part of the word.
3. Put the two parts together to read the word.

to / day = today

light / ning = lightning

dry / er = dryer

win / dow = window

be / fore = before

cray / on = crayon

ad / mire = admire

fa / ther = father

moth / er = mother

broth / er = brother

sis / ter = sister

    Success with Phonics: Letters and Sounds Workbook 8

Name _____   Date _____

Read-Write-Spell: Below are the names of the days of the week that you must learn. What do you do on these days?

Read Say the words	Write Trace the words	Spell Cover the first two columns, then spell the words
Sunday	Sunday	
Monday	Monday	
Tuesday	Tuesday	
Wednesday	Wednesday	
Thursday	Thursday	
Friday	Friday	
Saturday	Saturday	

Word List: Teachers! Parents! Below is a list of words with the letters and sounds taught in this workbook. The list also includes high frequency words. Have children read the words and use them to build sentences.

ay
day
may
way
say
play
stay

ea
meat
seat
read
meal
lead
teach

igh
light
right
fight
sight
night
bright

y
my
by
why
fly
cry
fry

ow, oe
low	hoe
row	foe
grow	toe
show	doe
blow	goes
elbow	aloe

ue
cue
due
sue
true
blue
glue

ew, ui
new	suit
dew	fruit
stew	cruise
blew	bruise
flew	juice
threw	

oi
oil
coil
join
point
spoil
moist

ou
round	**our**
mouth	**hour**
shout	sour
found	scour
ground	flour
noun	

Word List: Teachers! Parents! Below is a list of words with the letters and sounds taught in this workbook. The list also includes high frequency words. Have children read the words and use them to build sentences.

er

her
term
perm
verb
under
never

au

haul	**all**
Paul	ball
taunt	**call**
haunt	salt
fault	want
vault	**water**

are (air)

bare
care
dare
fare
share
scare

ere, eer

here	beer
mere	deer
there	jeer
where	cheer
sphere	steer
	queer

ire

fire
tire
wire
hire
empire
admire

ore

bore
core
more
chore
score
store

oar, oor

oar	**door**
boar	moor
soar	poor
roar	floor
board	spoor
hoard	

ure

pure
cure
mature
manure
endure

ph

phone
orphan
dolphin
Phillip
graphic
alphabet

Picture Cards: Copy the picture cards onto card stock paper. Color the borders and pictures on the cards. Cut them out and use them for a variety of literacy activities.

Made in the USA
Columbia, SC
03 July 2023

19756347R00024